PETROCHEMICAL ENGINEERING DIPLOMA & ENGINEERING MCQ

MANOJ DOLE

Contents

Foreword

Petrochemical Engineering Diploma & Engineering MCQ is a simple Book for Petrochemical Diploma & Engineering Course, It contains objective questions with underlined & bold correct answers MCQ covering all topics including all about the latest & Important about Petroleum Refining, Mechanical Engineering, Electrical and Electronics, Engineering, Mechanical Engineering and lots more.

We add new question answers with each new version. Please email us in case of any errors/omissions. This is arguably the largest and best e-Book for All engineering multiple choice questions and answers.

As a student you can use it for your exam prep. This e-Book is also useful for professors to refresh material.

Preface

This book may be purchased for educational, business, or sales promotional use. Online edition is also available for this title. For more information, contact our corporate/institutional sales department: [+919921582799] or [manojdole1@gmail.com]

While every precaution has been taken in the preparation of this book, the publisher and authors assume no responsibility for errors or omissions, or for damages resulting from the use of the information contained herein.

About the Author

MANOJ DOLE is an Engineer from reputed University. He is currently working with Government Industrial Training- Institute as a lecturer from last 12 Years. His interest include- Engineering Training Material, Invention & Engineering Practical- Knowledge etc.

CHAPTER ONE

Petrochemical Engineering Hand Tools & Measuring Instruments Theory

Download App
Online Test Exam
ITI Books
AutoCAD CAM
JOB & Apprentice
Online Theory
Computer Course
Trading Course
CNC Course
MSCIT Course
Shopping Business
Internet Business
Web Designing
Online Services
Top Sportsmans
Indian Army
Freedom Fighters
Top Scientists
Social Reformers
Motivational Speaker
Top Richest People
Join WhatsApp Group
Join Facebook Group
Like Facebook Page
PAN / Adhar / Licence Passport

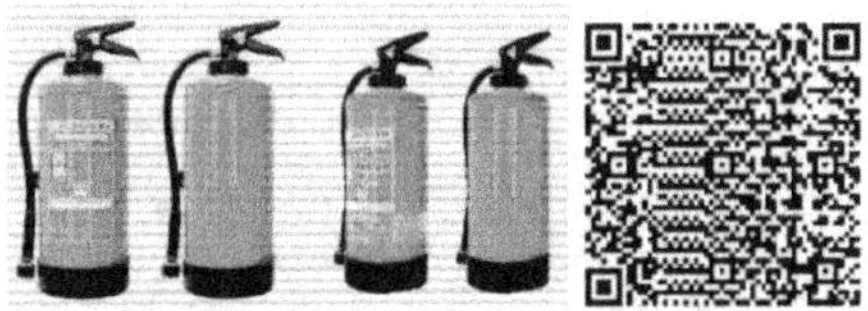
Fire extinguisher

Calliper

Hacksaw frame

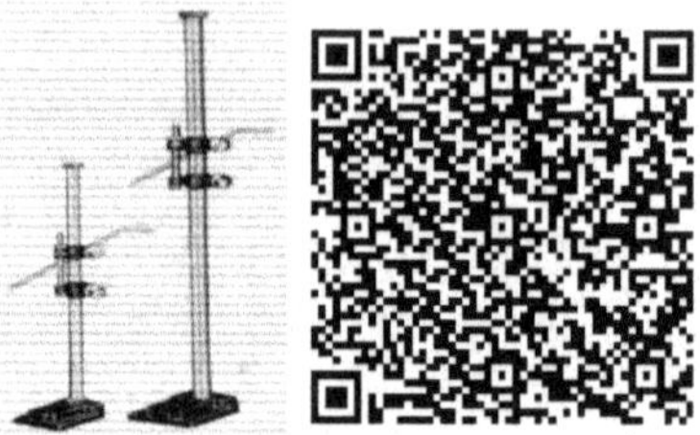

Universal surface guage

Hammer

Centre punch

Bench vice

Files

Scraper

Surface Plate

Outside Micrometer

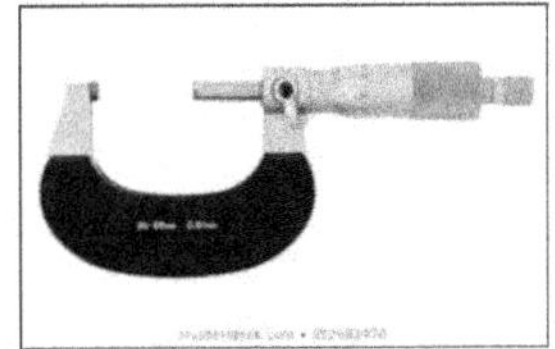

Micrometer

Depth micrometer

Vernier Calliper

Vernier bevel protractor

• 8 •

Drilling

Reamer

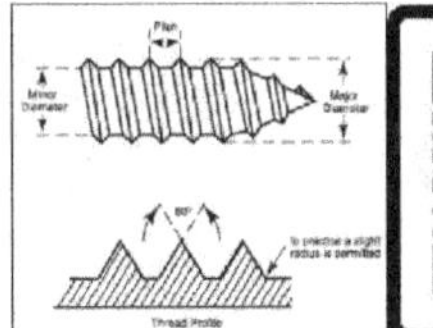

Thread

Tap Die

Grinding Wheel

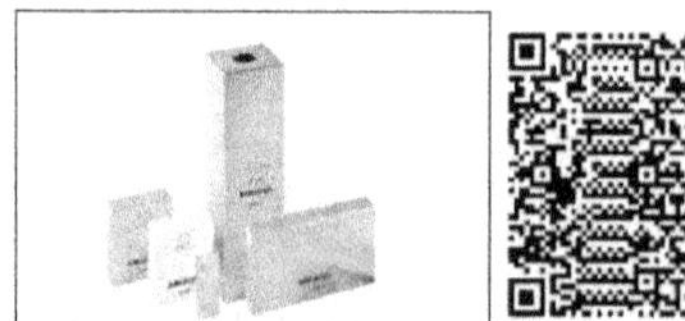

Slip gauge

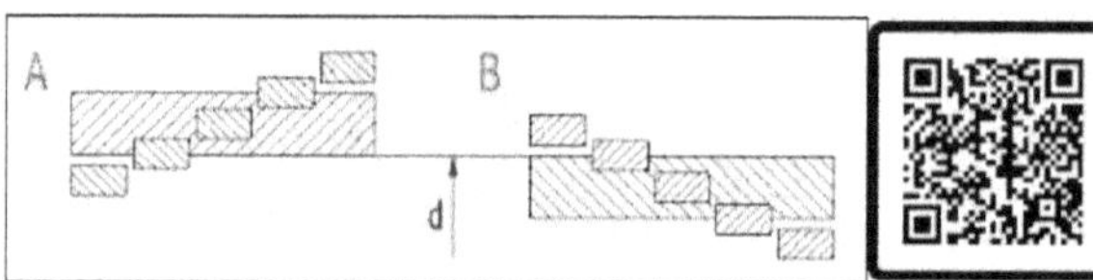

Limit fit tolerance

Lathe Machine

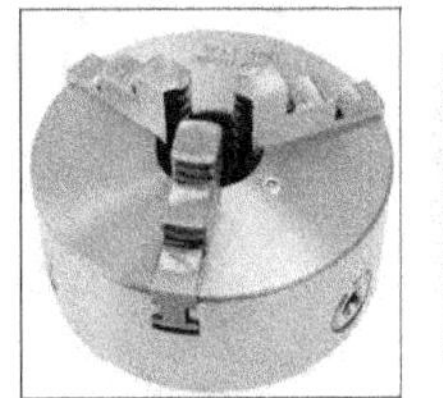

Lathe chuck

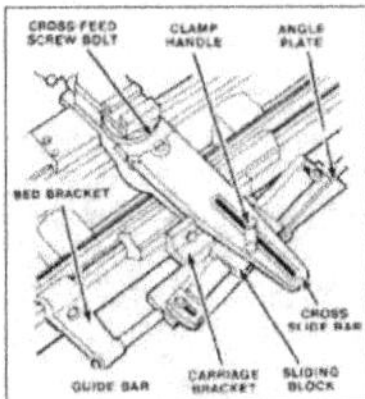

Taper turning attachment

taper ring gauge

screw pitch gauge

Gear

screw pitch gauge

Tap Die

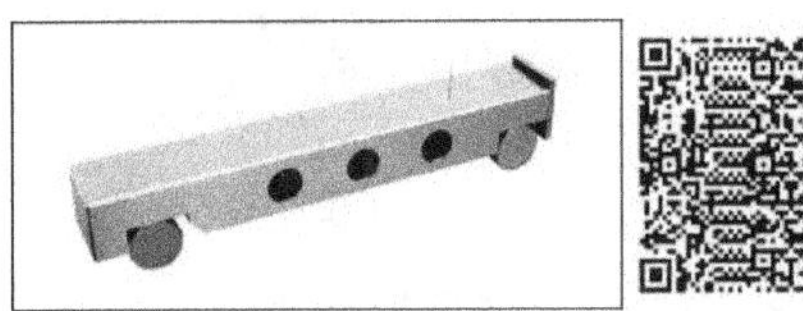

Sine bar

Slip gauge

Dial test indicator

Telescopic gauge

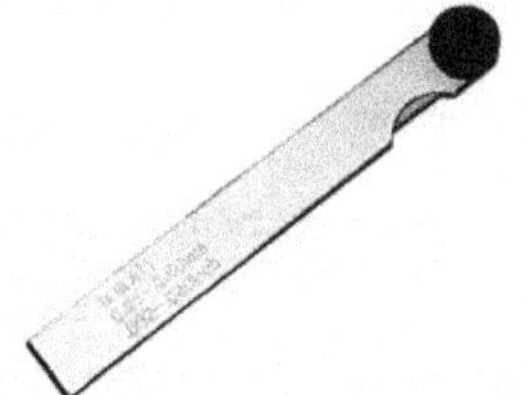 

Feeler gauge

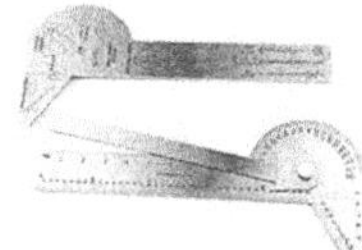 

Centre gauge

Jig

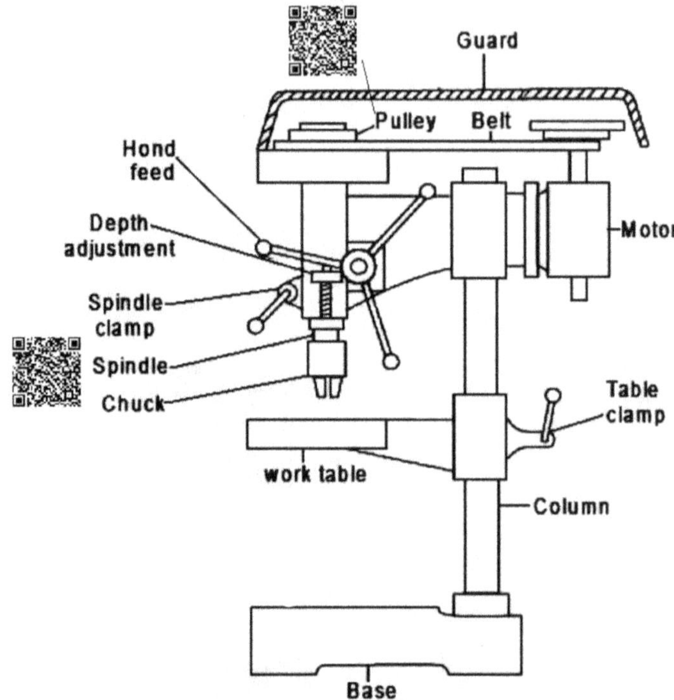

Piller Drilling Machine

Petrochemical Engineering Drawing Theory

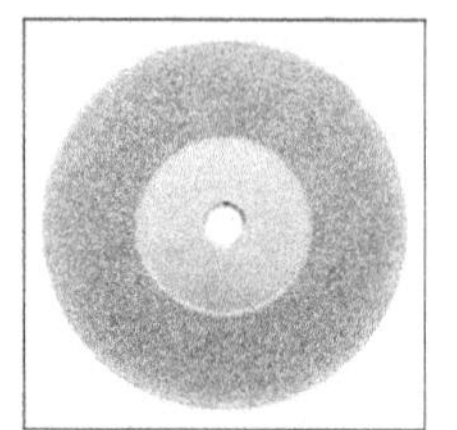

Grinding

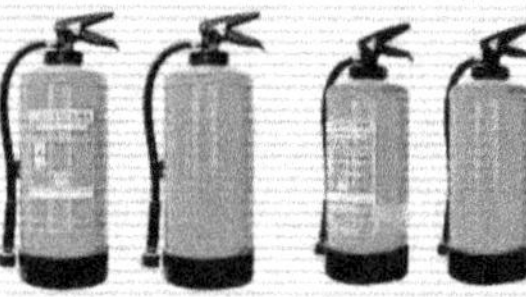

Fire extinguisher

French curve in drawing

Set square in drawing

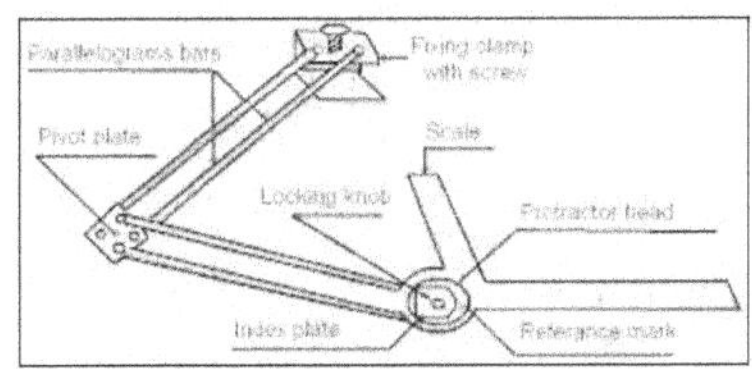

Mini drafter in drawing

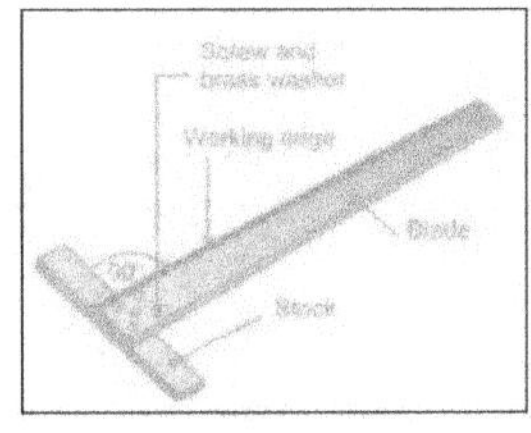

T - square in drawing

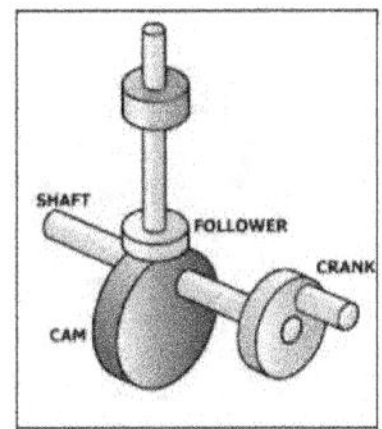

Cams in engine

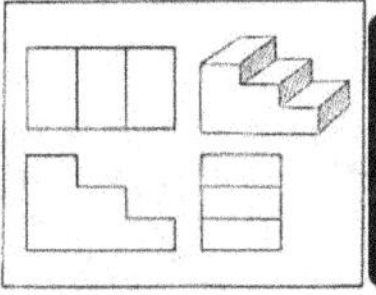

Orthographic projection in drawing

Third angle projection drawing

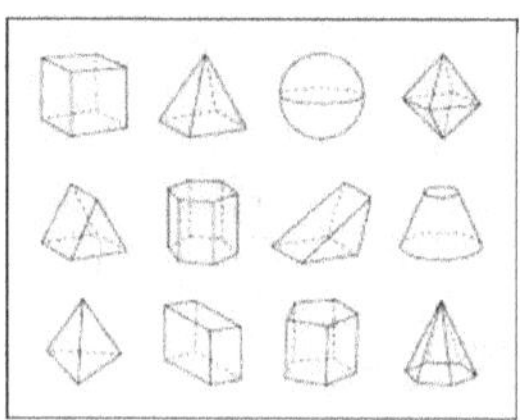

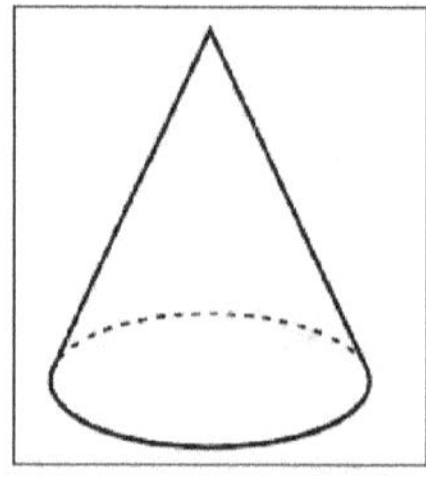

Cone in engineering drawing

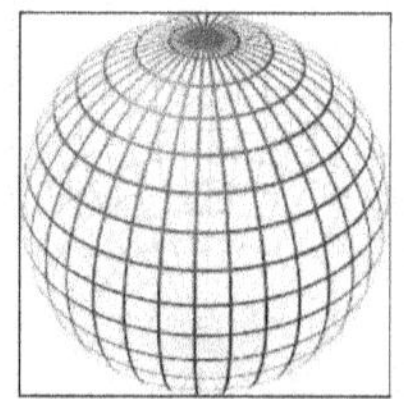

Sphere in drawing

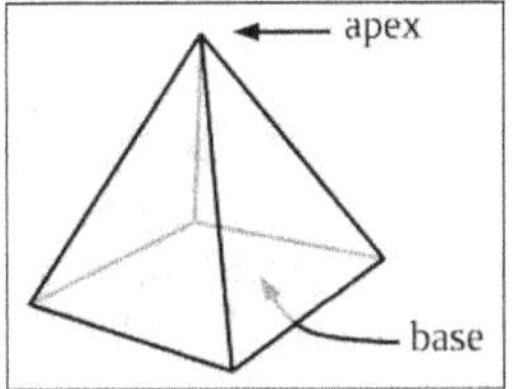

Pyramid drawing

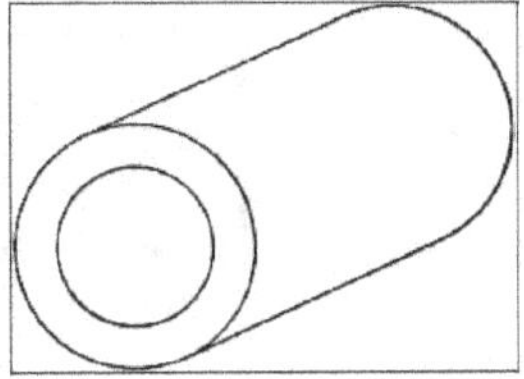

Cylinder in drawing

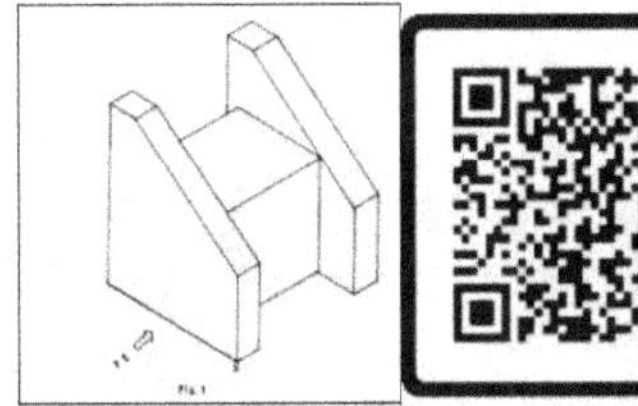

Isometric projections drawing

Curves engineering drawing

Sectional views in drawing

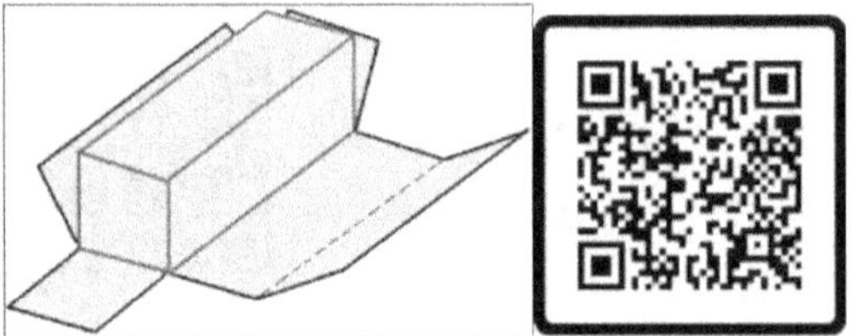

Development of surfaces in drawing

Hexagonal plane in drawing

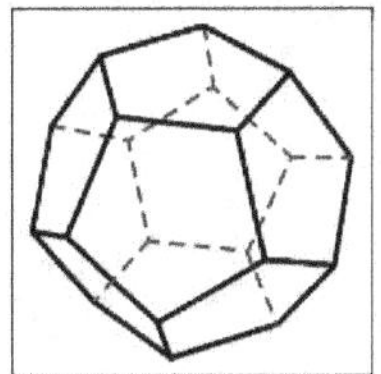

Polyhedron in drawing

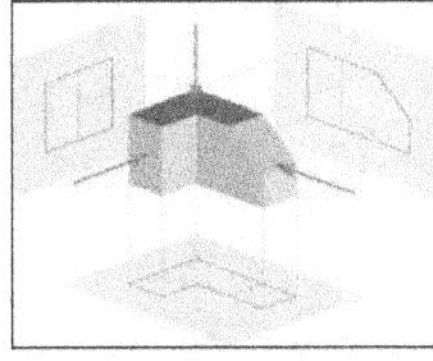

First Angle projection method in drawing

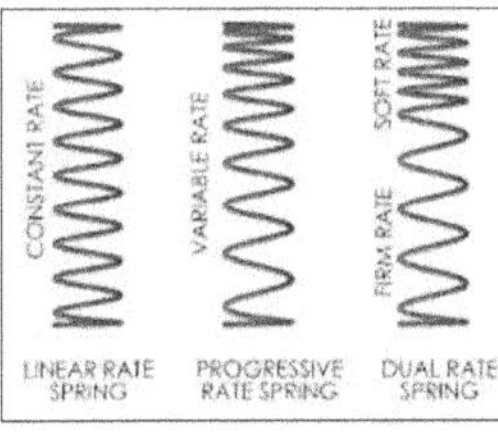

Springs in drawing

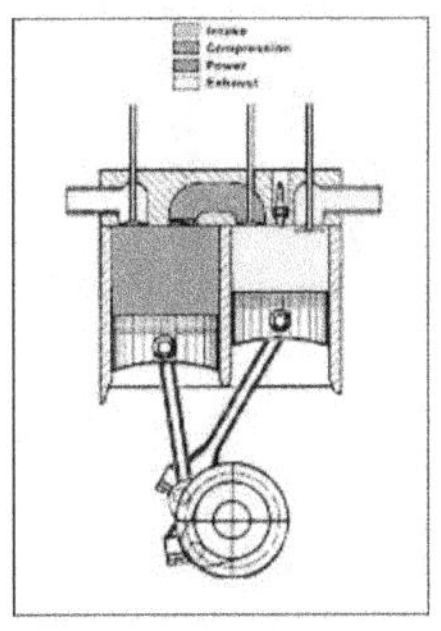

Engine in vehicle

CHAPTER THREE

Petrochemical Engineering Electrical Theory

battery
capacitor
cell
dynamometer
electromagnet
heater
inductance
magnet

15 ITI Book MCQ - Manoj Dole
www.itibook.com
megger
motor
multimeter
ohmmeter
resistores
star connected
alternator
voltmeter
ammeter
wattmeter
www.itigov.blogspot.com   www.jobapprentices.blogspot.com   www.ititests.blogspot.com
www.itibook.com

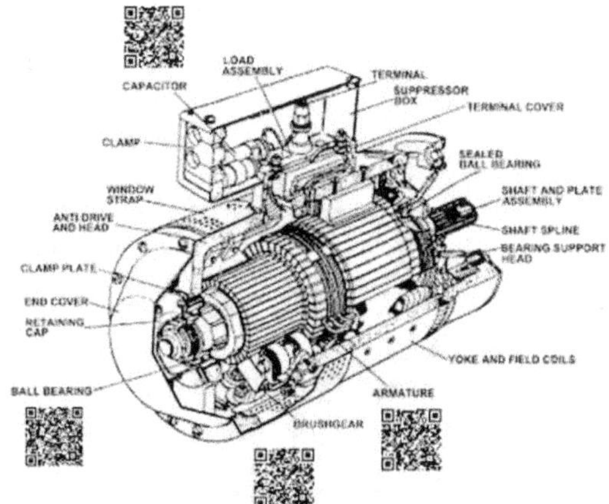

Electrical Generator

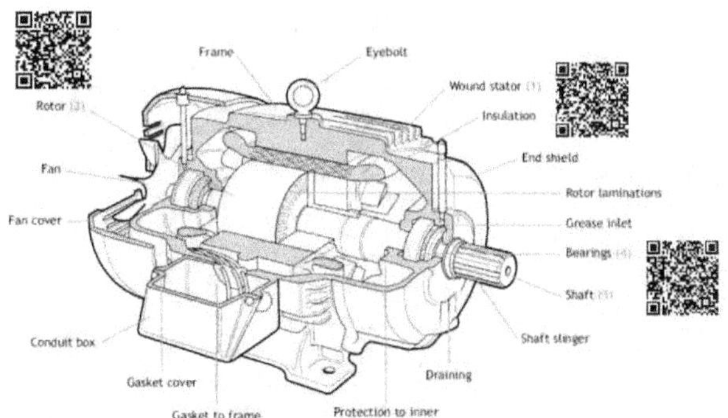

Electrical Induction Motor

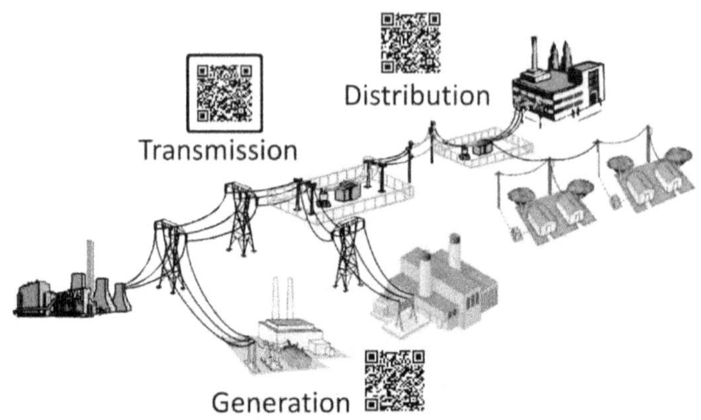

Electrical Power Distribution

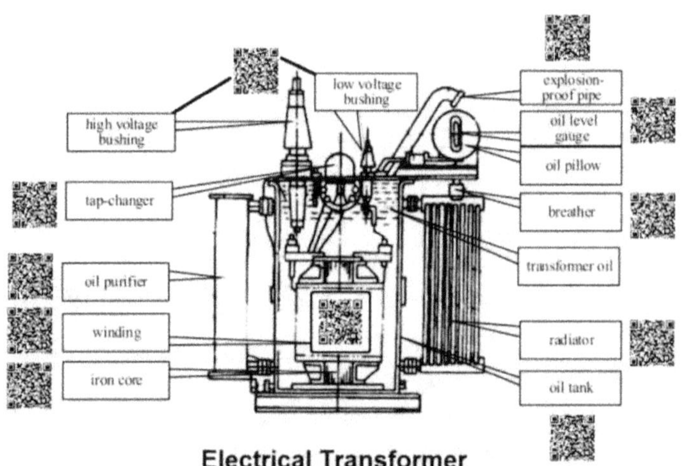

Electrical Transformer

CHAPTER FOUR

Petrochemical Engineering MCQ

Safety Precaution in Petrochemical Engineering

01] In case of bleeding, take treatment Of

A] spray cold water

B] Bandage immediately -----]

C] Enquire about the accident thought treatment

D] cold 3" and rest

02] in case of an accident, the victim should im

A] Asked to take rest

C] Attended immediately

D] leave him

03] First aid is given to an injured or ill person primarily....

A] Save life

B] Prevent further deterioration of the muff's

C] Give best possible comfort

D] All of these

04] Colour code for Bins for waste paper segregation is -----

A] blue Colour

B] Yellow Colour

C] Red Colour

D] Green Colour

05] In Japanese Seiko stands for --------------

A] Shine

B] Sort

C] Standardize

D] Sustain

06] Benefit of SS system is ------

A] Increase in productivity

B] Increase in quality

C] Reduction in wastage of time

D] All of these

07] Safety is -----------

A] nobody's business

B] every bodise business

C] Some bodies business

D] The organization business

08] For basic categories of safety signs are available The meaning of"prohibition" sign ----

A] shows it must not be done

B] Shows what must be done

C] Warns the hazard or danger

D] Gives information of safety provision

09] Which one is a workshop safety?

A] Keep shop floor clean and free from grease, oil or other slippery materials

B] Stop the machine before changing the speed

C] Don't use cracked or chipped tools

D] Don't try to stop a running machine with hand

10] In Personal Protect Equipment (PPE] HELMET is used to

A] protect head

B] Protect eyes

C] Protect hands

D] Protect ears

11] Which of the following belongs to general safety?

A Have a worker in good attitude

B] The work clean and clear

C] Concentrate on your work

D] Keep the floor and gangways clean and clear

12] While grinding, which is used to protect the eyes?

A] Dark green glass

B] Mask

C] Sun glasses

D] Safety goggles

13] Which of the following is done for machine safety?

A] Check the oil level before starting the machine

B] Do things in a methodical way

C] Keep the floor and gangways clean and clear

D] Don't use dies and scarves

14] In Personal Protect Equipment (PPE], 'sleeves' is used to protect ----------

A] Face

B] Eyes

C] Ears

D] Hands

15] ABC stands for --------------

A] Automatic Breathing Control

B] Automatic Blood Control

C] Airway Breathing Circulation

D] Automatic Blood Circulation

16] To put off"Class B" fire, the types of fire extinguisher used is ....]

A] dry power

B] Carbon dioxide

C] Jet of water

D] Foam type

17] Which type of fire extinguisher is used to put off general fire?

A] Water type Extinguisher

B] Foam type Extinguisher

C] Dry chemical powder Extinguisher

D] Carbon dioxide (C02] Extinguisher

Hand Tools in Petrochemical Engineering

18] One micrometer (U] is equal to...

A] 0.1mm

B] 0.01mm

C] 0.001mm

D] 0.0001mm

19] Name the tool used to make and finish the leak proof joints of a pipe T joint

A] groover

B] setting hammer

C] creasing hammer

D] round bottom stake

20] Portion of the hammer used for fixing the handle is...

A] Face

B] Peen

C] Cheek

D] <u>Eye hole</u>

21] Weight of the hammer for the marking purpose is...

A] <u>250g</u>

B] 500g

C] 1 kg

D] 2 kgs

22] To cut out small apertures which punch and die type of machine is used?

A] shear type nibbler

B] <u>punch type nibbler</u>

C] circular cutting machine

D] guillotine shearing machine

23] Scribers are made of...

A] Mild steel

B] <u>High carbon steel</u>

C] Brass

D] Cast iron

24] The size of an engineer's vice is specified by the...

A] Length of the movable jaw

B] <u>Width of the jaws</u>

C] Height of the vice

D] Maximum opening of the jaws

vice   Bench vice

Bench Vice

25] The form of thread used in carpenters vice is...

A] Square

B] <u>Acme thread</u>

C] <u>Sawtooth Thread</u>

D] Knuckle thread

26] The convexity of files helps...

A] To file concave surfaces

B] To file convex surfaces

C] <u>To prevent rounding of edges of work</u>

D] The file to become straight when pressure is applied

27]] Name the instrument used to check the perpendicularity of the branch pipe with the main pipe of a pipe T joint

A] protractor

B] <u>try square</u>

C] spirit level

D] straight edge

28] The caliper meant for measuring the width of a slot is...

A] Odd leg caliper

B] Outside caliper

C] Jenny caliper

D] <u>Inside calliper</u>

29] The included angle of the groove of 'V' block is always....

A] 45°

B] 60°

C] 90°

D] <u>120°</u>

<u>v blocks</u>

<u>v block</u>

'V' blocks

30] 'V' blocks are available in grades of...

A] <u>A & B</u>

B] A,B & C

C] 1,2 & 3

D] 1 & 2

31] 'V' blocks of grade 'B' are made of

A] <u>Cast iron</u>

B] Mild steel

C] Steel

D] Cast steel

32] 'V' block 50/5-40 A is used for holding jobs of diameter

A] Ø 50 mm

B] Ø 5 to Ø 50 mm

C] <u>Ø 5 to Ø 40 mm</u>

D] Ø 40 mm

33] The reason for using cast iron in making 'V' blocks

A] to increase the weight of the block

B] to reduce the cost

C] to reduce the friction

D] to get a good appearance

34] For cutting thin tubing, the most suitable pitch of the hacksaw blade is...

A] 1.8mm

B] 1.4mm

C] 1mm

D] 0.8mm

35] For cutting solid brass, the most suitable pitch of the hacksaw blade is...

A] 1.8mm

B] 1.4mm

C] 1mm

D] 0.8mm

36] A new hacksaw blade after a few strokes becomes loose because of the...

A] Stretching of the blade

B] Wing-nut threads being worn out

C] Wrong pitch of the blade

D] Improper selection of the set of saws.

37] While cutting small diameter pipes, it is advisable to watch regularly and ensure that...

A] The cut is along the curved line

B] More saw teeth are in contract

C] The work is not overheated

D] Proper balancing of hacksaw is maintained

Drilling in Petrochemical Engineering

38] If the drill runs untrue, it will

A] get too hot

B] cut undersize

C] distort the spindle

D] cut an oversized hole

39] Running the drill too fast many result in

A] spoiling the cutting edge

B] poor surface finish

C] twisting the tang

D] drilling an oval hole

40] A drill with worn land will
A] drill hole oversize
B] <u>drill hole undersize</u>
C] run out of centre
D] drill an accurate hole
41] The morse taper provided on drills used on lathe ranges between
A] <u>MT1 to MT5</u>
B] MT1 to MT4
C] MT0 to MT5
D] MT0 to MT4
42] Feeding the small drill too fast into the work may result in
A] <u>breaking the drill</u>
B] bending the drill
C] cutting an oval shape hole
D] increased production
43] The drill size for a M 20 tap is
A] <u>17.5 mm</u>
B] 18 mm
C] 18.5 mm
D] 19 mm
44] The taper shank drills are held on the machine by means of...
A] Chucks
B] <u>Sleeves</u>
C] Drift
D] Vice
45] Drill chucks are fitted on the drilling machine spindle by means of a...
A] Knurled ring
B] <u>Arbor</u>
C] Drift
D] Pinion and key

drill chuck

drilling

Drill Chuck

46] The Morse taper provided on drills ranges between...

A] <u>MT 1 to MT 5</u>

B] MT 1 to MT 4

C] MT 0 to MT 5

D] MT 0 to MT 4

47] A drift is used for...

A] Drawing a drill location

B] Fixing chuck on the machine spindle

C] Removing a broken drill from the work

D] <u>Removing the drill from the machine spindle</u>

48] When the taper shank of the drill is larger than the machine spindle, the device to hold the drill is a...

A] Drill sleeve

B] <u>Taper socket</u>

C] Drill drift

D] Chuck and key

49] A special feature of the radial drilling machine is...

A] It can be used for drilling with a H.S.S] drill
B] Table can be moved and set at any position
C] A variety of speeds is available
D] <u>The spindle can be brought to any position</u>
50] The point angle of drills depends on...
A] The size of the drill
B] The type of machine
C] <u>The material of the work</u>
D] The RPM of the drill
51] The point angle for a standard drill is...
A] 60°
B] 108°
C] <u>118°</u>
D] 135°
52] The helical angle determines the...
A] Cutting angle
B] Chew angle
C] <u>Rake angle</u>
D] Lip angle
53] The clearance angle of the drill is between...
A] 3° to 5°
B] <u>8° to 12°</u>
C] 12° to 20°
D] 15° to 20°
54] The relief angle provided behind the cutting edge is called the..
A] Point angle
B] Chisel edge angle
C] Helix angle
D] <u>Clearance angle</u>
55] A set of number drill series consists of drills in the following ranges]
Indicate the correct range
A] 1 to 40
B] 1 to 50
C] <u>1 to 80</u>
D] 1 to 100
56] In the number drill series, the smallest drill size is...
A] 0.1 mm

B] <u>0.35 mm</u>
C] 0.5 mm
D] 0.52 mm
57] In the number drill series, the largest drill size is...
A] 102 mm
B] <u>5.791 mm</u>
C] 5.613 mm
D] 5.410 mm
58] In the letter drill series, the size of the drill 'A' is equal to ...
A] 13 mm
B] 6.08 mm
C] 6.045 mm
D] <u>5.944 mm</u>
59] In the letter drill series, the largest drill size is equal to...
A] 10.33 mm
B] <u>10.490 mm</u>
C] 12.01 mm
D] 15.00 mm
60] In a remote place (no electricity available] a rail track is to be drilled] Choose the right drilling machine
A] Radial drilling machine
B] Pillar drilling machine
C] <u>Ratchet drilling machine</u>
D] Sensitive drilling Machine
61] A drilling machine used by a carpenter for cabinet making is a...
A] Ratchet drilling machine
B] Radial drilling machine
C] <u>Breast drilling machine</u>
D] Sensitive drilling machine
62] Surface plates are made of...
A] High grade cast steel
B] <u>Fine-grained cast iron</u>
C] Alloy steels
D] Wrought iron
63] The drill size for a M 20 tap is
A] <u>17.5 mm</u>
B] 18 mm
C] 18.5 mm

D] 19 mm

64] Tapping is mostly done to produce

A] external 'V' thread

B] <u>internal 'V' thread</u>

C] external square thread

D] internal square thread

65] The drill size for tapping is

A] more than the tap size

B] <u>less than the tap size</u>

C] equal to the tap size

D] either more or less than the tap size

66] which one of the following is the most suitable tap for lathe work?

A] spiral tap

B] <u>machine tap</u>

C] hand tap

D] left hand tap

67] A die is turned with a

A] die wrench

B] <u>diestock</u>

C] die plate

D] die handle

68] A tumbler gear unit has

A] a single gear

B] two gears

C] <u>three gears</u>

D] four gears

69] The cutting edge of a solid tool is made of

A] <u>carbon steel</u>

B] mild steel

C] super high speed steel

D] stelite

70] The tip of a cemented carbide threading tool is

A] <u>brazed</u>

B] welded

C] soldered

D] clamped to the shank

71] Tool will rub against the work surfaces and the cutting force increases when..

A] The clearance angle is more
B] The clearance angel is less
C] The rake angle is more
D] The rake angle is less
72] Formation of a chip while cutting is based on the...
A] Rake angle of the tool
B] Clearance angle of the tool
C] Wedge angle of the tool
D] Clearance and wedge angle of the tool
73] The suitable cutting fluid for drilling mild steel in a drilling machine is...
A] Synthetic soluble oil
B] Neat oil
C] Distilled water
D] Soluble oil
74] Centre drilling is an operation of...
A] Drilling and countersinking
B] Drilling and counter boring
C] Marking the centre location before drilling
D] Enlarging the diameter of a hole
75] Shaft ends are centre drilled for...
A] Supporting jobs between centres
B] Lubricating the dead centre
C] Reducing the weight
D] Assisting counter boring
76] The Centre drill size is selected on the basis of the
A] length of the job
B] material of the job
C] diameter of the job
D] type of operation
77] Centre drilling is done at a
A] high spindle speed with a high feed
B] low spindle speed with a high feed
C] high spindle speed with a low feed
D] low spindle speed with a low feed
Measuring Instruments in Petrochemical Engineering
78] The least count of vernier caliper is
A] 0.01 mm

B] <u>0.02mm</u>
C] 0.001 mm
D] 0.2 mm

vernier caliper

vernier caliper

Vernier Caliper

79] The graduations of a depth micrometer are...

A] Similar to an outside micrometer

B] <u>In the reverse direction to that of the outside micrometer, both Thimble and sleeve</u>

C] In the reverse direction only on the sleeve

D] In the direction only on the thimble

depth micrometer

depth micrometer

Depth Micrometer

80] The process of enlarging the end of a hole for accommodating the socket screw head is...

A] Reaming
B] Spot facing
C] <u>Counter boring</u>
D] Counter sinking

boring

Boring Operation

81]While choosing a boring tool for boring a given diameter, select

A] a long tool

B] a short tool

C] a long and stout tool

D] a short and stout tool

82] The cutting edge of the boring tool should be set for a small hole so that it is

A] 0.5 mm above the center

B] 0.5 mm below the center

C] 1 mm above the center

D] in the exact center

83] Bored holes are to be chamfered by using

A] a drill

B] triangular scraper

C] a cranked boring tool

D] a flat file

84] The tool used for boring deep holes is a

A] lathe mandrel

B] sleeve

C] drill

D] boring bar

E] auger bit

85] The cutting speed for rough boring is the

A] same as rough turning

B] same as drilling

C] same as knurling

D] same as thread cutting

86] The reamer is used for...

A] Drilling holes in thin sheets

B] Drilling deep holes

C] Removing burrs

D] Enlarging and finishing holes

reamer

reamer

Reamer

87] The reamer teeth are unevenly spaced because...
A] They are easy to manufacture
B] <u>They can reduce chattering</u>
C] They help to cut metal gradually
D] They help to remove the reamer easily
88] Which among the following is not a capability of reamers?
A] Finishing small holes
B] <u>Finishing any machined profiles</u>
C] Accuracy to closer limits
D] Producing high quality surface finish
89] The most important quality of any cutting fluid is
A] emulsification
B] specific heat
C] specific gravity
D] <u>viscosity</u>

cutting fluid 1

Cutting Fluid

90] By using coolants on workpieces we can choose
A] higher cutting speeds
B] lower cutting feeds
C] lower cutting speeds
D] heavy depth of cuts
91] The cutting speed for aluminium with H.S.S] tools is
A] 30 m/min
B] 50 m/min
C] 70 m/min
D] 130 m/min
92] The cutting speed for brass with a H.S.S] tool is
A] 10 m/min
B] 25 m/min
C] 70 m/min
D] 140 m/min
93] The distance, which the cutting edge of a tool passes over the material in a minute while machining is Know as...
A] RPM
B] Feed
C] Machine speed
D] Cutting speed
94] The cutting angle for chipping cast iron is...
A] 37.5°
B] 55°
C] 60°
D] 90°
95] The depth of cut is given by

A] the top slide
B] the cross-slide
C] the compound slide
D] adjusting the tool
96] For mounting a lathe chuck
A] start it by hand and then turn the power on
B] mount it on by power
C] mount it by hand
D] mount it with the help of a hammer

lathe chucks

lathe chuck

Lathe Four Jaw Chuck
97] The morse taper provided on drills used on lathe ranges between
A] MT1 to MT5
B] MT1 to MT4
C] MT0 to MT5
D] MT0 to MT4
98] Feeding the small drill too fast into the work may result in
A] breaking the drill
B] bending the drill

C] cutting an oval shape hole

D] increased production

99] Number of flutes in a twist drills are --------

A] 1

B] 2

C] 3

D] 4

100] Which one of the following drilling machines is used for drilling holes where electricity is not available?

A] Bench drilling machine

B] Pillar drilling machine

C] Redial drilling machine

D] Ratchet drilling machine

101] Which one of the following drilling machine is used for heavy duty work?

A] Bench drilling machine

B] Pillar drilling machine

C] Radial drilling machine

D] Electric hand drilling machine

102] The suitable cutting fluid for drilling mild steel in a lathe is

A] synthetic soluble oil

B] neat cutting oil

C] distilled water

D] soluble oil+water

103] The suitable cutting fluid for precision grinding is

A] Soluble oil

B] Synthetic soluble oil

C] Neat oil

D] Servo Cut's'

gringing wheel   grinding wheel

Grinding Wheel

104] Advantage of using cutting fluid during grinding operation is ------

A] 5000 surface finish

B] Reduction in cutting forces

C] Reduction in hardening of the work piece

D] All of these]

105] Lubricant is necessary to ....]

A] run the machine smoothly taking least load

B] Run the machine quickly

C] Stop the machine immediately

D] Produce work piece of greater accuracy

106] The main purpose for using a lubricant in machine tools is to ------

A] Cool down the making parts

B] Prevent machine tool from heating

C] Wet the making parts for close contact

D] Minimize the friction between the making parts

107] Driving plates are used for

A] mounting fixtures and workpieces

B] driving shafts between Centre's with a lathe dog

C] facing operations only

D] internal operations only

108] Balancing is done in the face plate work

A] to increase the speed

B] to reduce the pressure on the tool

C] for uniform rotation of work

D] to get a good finish

109] A face plate is used to hold

A] a round job

B] a finished job

C] an irregular Job

D] a hollow job

110] Which is correct angle plate used with face plate

(A] Solid Type

(B] Box Type

(C] Adjustable Type

(D] None of them

angle plate

Angle Plate

111] Face plate is made from.....]
(A] Mild Steel
(B] Cast Iron
(C] Brass
(D] Aluminium
112] Which following accessories is use for odd an uneven job turning?
(A] Three Jaw Chuck
(B] Two Jaw Chuck
(C] Driving Plate
(D] Face Plate
113] An irregular shaped work piece is turned on a Lathe] Which one of the following work holding accessories is used?
A] Two Jaw chuck
B] Three Jaw chuck
C] Driving plate
D] Face plate
114]The pads of a steady rest are made of
A] carbon steel
B] lead
C] mild steel
D] brass

steady rest

• 51 •

Steady Rest

115] A steady rest is used
A] to hold jobs
B] for face plate work
C] to drive the job
D] to support the job
116] A follower steady is held on the
A] lathe bed
B] lathe carriage
C] lathe spindle
D] tailstock
117] When turning long work pieces, the following is used
A sleeve
B change gear
C steady rest
D bracket]
118] Knurling operation is done at the
A] turning spindle speed
B] high spindle speed
C] 1/3 of the turning spindle speed
D] 1/2 of the turning spindle speed

knurling tool

Knurling Tool

119] Knurling is the operation of

A] shearing

B] <u>forming</u>

C] turning

D] pressing

120] Mandrels are generally used when machining with

A] heavy cuts

B] <u>short facing cuts</u>

C] light cuts

D] boring tools

Limit Fit & Tolerances in Petrochemical Engineering

121] In the B.I.S system 25 hole deviations are specified by

A] small letters

B] small letters with numbers

C] small letters with tolerance

D] <u>capital letters</u>

122] The standard range of sizes covered in the B.I.S] system of limits and fits are

A] 0 to 10 mm

B] 0 to 100 mm

C] <u>25 to 400 mm</u>

D] 0 to 500 mm

123] The basic size is the size

A] mentioned in the drawing

B] machined by the operator

C] <u>based on which deviations are given</u>

D] given by the instructor

124] Limits of size are

A] 2

B] 3

C] 4

D] 5

125] The number of fundamental deviations in the B.I.S] system are

A] 20

B] 22

C] 25

D] 28

126] The number of grade of tolerances in the B.I.S] system are

A] 12

B] 16

C] 18

D] 20

127] The size based on which the dimensional deviations are given is called...

A] Actual size

B] Basic size

C] Minimum limit of size

D] Maximum limit of Size

128] The size of parts made by .....] for provide interchange ability properties] (A] Measurement System

(B] Trial and Error System

(C] Limit and Tolerance System

(D] None of Them

129] Your job taper is correct if it is measured

A above the higher limit

B in between higher and lower limit

C below the lower limit]

130] When tolerance given in one side of the basic dimension, it is called ---------

A].Tolerance system

B] Unilateral tolerance

C] Bilateral tolerance

D] Allowance System

131] A dimension is stated as (025 H7 in a drawing] The lower limit is -----------

A] 24.75 mm

B] 24.85 mm

C] 25.00 mm

D] 25-021 mm

132] The measured Size Of the dimensions of a component as called---------

A] Basic size

B] Nominal Size

C] Allowed size

D] Actual size

133] In the drawing the dimensions of a shaft is shown 40i 0068/0042, which is the size of Shaft within the tolerance?

A] 4.0.64 mm

B] 40.042 mm

C] 40.000 mm

D] 39.998 mm

134] In Hole basic system ----------

A] The size of the shaft is made constant

B] The Size of the hole is made constant

C] Only 'allowance is given on the hole

D] The permissible tolerance are given on the hole and the Shaft

135] The Size of a component is given as 24 -0.1] What does -O.1 indicates? _

A] Upper deviation is + 0.1 mm]

B] Lower deviation is 0.0 mm

C] Fundamental deviation is 0.0 mm

D] Lower deviation is _0.1 mm

136] The tolerance of a hole iS the difference between the -------

A] Maximum hole Size and maximum Shaft size

B] Maximum hole size and maximum hole Size

C] Minimum'hole size and maximum Shaft Size

D] Minimum hole Size and minimum shaft Size

137] A hole whose lower deviation is zero is called basic hole] Which one of the following letter indicates basic hole?]

A] E

B] F

C] G '

D] H

138] Which one having upper deviation zero?
A] Bassc Shaft
B] Basic hole
C] Tolerance
D] Clearance
139] A ball bearing on a shaft is type of fit? ,
A] Clearance fit
B] Driving fit
C] Shrinkage fit
D] None of the above
140] Which one of the following is important factor required to achieve the interchange ability in mass production?]
A] Geometrical accuracy]
B] Standardization
C] Dimensional accuracy
D] Surface finish
141] In the BIS system of limits and fits, the grade of tolerance are represented by number Symbols and there are ---------i
A] 14 grades of tolerance
B] 16 grades of tolerance
C] 18 grades of tolerance '
D] 20 grades of tolerance
142] A Product is said to have the quality when ....]
A] Its shape and dimensions are within the limit
B] It is fit for use
C] It appears to be very good
D] The choice of material is right
143] The maximum clearance required between hole'30 +0.021, 0.000 and shaft 30 -0.110, 0.143 is.
A] 0.110 mm '
B]0.131 mm
C] 0.164 mm
D] 0.143 mm
144] A dimension is stated as 25 .1002 mm in a drawing] What is the tolerance?
A] +0.02 mm'
B] +0.04 mm
C] -0.02 mm

D] 25.00 mm

145] A pin is fitted in a hole] The tolerance zone of the pin is entirely above that of hole] The fit obtained will be?

A] Clearance fit

B] Transition fit

C] Interference fit

D] Running fit

146] Interchange ability is normally applied for? _

A] Repairing of parts

B] Mass production

C] Single piece production

D] All of these

147] Tolerance is given to the part size to...........]

A] Production the part within the required permissible size error

B] Increase the production

C] Decrease the Production

D] Finish the components approximately

148] Which one of the following is the clearance fit under the whole basic system?

A] 20 H7/p6'

B] 2067/211

C] ZOG/gll]

D] 20H/g11]

149] The three classes of fits as per BIS system aré ....] ~]

A] Clearance fit, interference fit and transition fit

B] Medium fit, push fit and tight fit

C] Flat fit, round fit and square fit

D] 'Sliding fit ', loose fit and shrinkage fit

150] Which one of the following tolerance specifications has a maximum dimensionless than 20 mm?

A] 20 +0.2,-0.3

B] 20 320.2

C] 20 -0.2, 0.3 e

D]m 20 +500, ~03

151] Difference between the maximum and minimum limit is -~-~~~~~- ~~~~~ '

A] Single informant

B] Basic shaft

C] Clearance

D] <u>Tolerance</u>

152] A shaft 55 running freely in bush bearing the type of fit is ---------

A] Clearance fit

B] Driving plate

C] <u>shrinkage fit</u>

D] None of the above

153] The taper ratio of the morse taper is

A] 1 in 10

B] 1 in 15

C] <u>1 in 20</u>

D] 1 in 25

154] The morse standard taper is available in

A] 16 Nos

B] 12 Nos

C] <u>10 Nos</u>

D] 8 Nos

155] Taper turning by offsetting the tailstock method can produce

A] an internal taper

B] an internal taper thread

C] <u>an external taper</u>

D] both external and internal tapers

taper turning

taper turning attachment

Taper by Tailstock Offset

156] By using the taper turning attachment, tapers can be turned with a setting angle up to

A] 10°

B] <u>15°</u>

C] 20°

D] 30°

157] The accuracy of a taper is generally checked by means of......

A] taper gauges

B] gauge blocks

C] indicator and height gauge

D] 'V' blocks

158] Turning tapers by the compound rest method involves working solely with

Decimal measurements

B fractional measurements

C metric measurements

D angular measurements]

159] Long tapers are produced

A with the taper turning attachment

B with the compound slide

C by setting over the tail stock

D by adjusting the cross slide]

160] The length of turned tapers are checked with

A vernier calliper

B micrometer

C inside callper

D dial test indicator]

161] The disadvantages of taper turning using the com] pound slide are

A] only long tapers can be turned

B] only very large tapers can be turned

C] only manual in feed is possible

D] only short tapers can be turned due to the restrictions of the compound slide]

162] External tapers are checked with

A] limit plug gauge

B] taper ring gauge

C]taper plug gauge

D] thread plug gauge]

163] The use of a taper turned on lathe is ----

A] Assist to transmit drive in the assembled parts

B] Used for Assembly and disassembly of parts

C] Give self alignment in the assembled parts

164] Which type of method is used in mass production of production of producing small length of taper?

A] Form tool

B] Compound slide

C] Tailstock offset.

D] Taper turning attachment

165] Morse standard taper is one of the internationally accepted standards taper, which is available in numbers from--------

A]1to7

B]1 to 8

C] O to 7

D] 0 to 8

166] Which taper turning method is used for cutting steep taper?

A] Set over method

B] Taper turning attachment

C] Form tool

D] Swivelling the compound rest

167] Morse taper is used in which of the following machine components -...

A] Spindles of lathe

B] Spindles of drill machine

C] Shanks of reamers

D] All of these

168] For mass production of the taper which one of the following method is used.......]

A] Tailstock offset method

B] Taper turning attachment method

C] Form too method

D] Compound slide method

169] The major diameter of the taper is 40 mm, minor diameter is 30 mm] The total length of the job is 100 mm is tapered then offset is given by -

A] 5 mm

B] 7.5 mm

C] 12 mm

D] 9 mm

170] The accuracy of an ordinary bevel protractor is --' ------------degree]

A] One

B] Three

C] Two

D] Four

171] The least count of a vernier bevel protractor is...

A] 1"

B] <u>5'</u>

C] 1°

D] 5 °

172] The part of a vernier bevel protractor which is normally used as a reference base for measuring angles is the...

A] Blade

B] <u>Stock</u>

C] Disc

C] Main scale

173] The part of a vernier bevel protector on which main scale divisions are marked is the...

A] Stock

B] Dial

C] <u>Disc</u>

D] Adjustable blade

174] The part of a bevel protractor, which comes in contact with the inclined surface while measuring is the...

A] <u>Blade</u>

B] Stock

C] Disc

D] Dial

175] The value of each division of the main scale of a vernier bevel protractor is...

A] 5'

B] <u>1°</u>

C] 5°

D.10°

176] The value of each division of the vernier scale of a bevel protractor is...

A] 1°

B] 1°5'

C] <u>1°55'</u>

D.5'

177] The part of the vernier bevel protractor on which main scale divisions are marked

A stock

B dial

C disc

D adjustable blade

178] In Vernier bevel protractor is designed to measure?

A] Acute angles

B] Obtuse angles

C] Acute and Obtuse angle

D] Liner dimensions

179] To get least count of 5 in a vernier bevel protractor the 23° main scale are divided into -..

A] 12 equal parts on vernier scale

B] 22 equal parts on vernier scale

C] 24 equal parts on vernier scale

D] 25 equal parts on vernier scale

180] Which of the following is not the part of a combination set?

A] Stock

B] Square head

C] Protractor head

D] Centre head

181] The datum, form which the measurements of the vernier height gauge are taken, is...

A] The beam

B] The vernier slide

C] The base

D] Above the scriber poing

vernier height gauge

vernier height guage

Vernier Height Gauge

182] The part of a vernier height gauge on which the main scale divisions are graduated is the...

A] Base

B] <u>Beam</u>

C] Fine setting device

D] The vernier plate

183] On which part of the vernier height gauge are the main scale division graduated?]

A] Base

B] Vernier plate

C] <u>Beam</u>

D] Fine adjusting unit

184] For marking purpose a Vernier height gauge must be on the --------

A] Bed of a machine tool

B] <u>Surface plate</u>

C] Square block

D] Any flat surface

185] Before using Vernier height gauge make sure that the --------

A] Locking screw is in a locked position

B] Scriber is Locked

C] <u>Zero of the vernier coincides with zero of the main scale</u>

D] Gib is Provided

186] The least count Of a vernier height gauge is...........]

A] 0.05 mm

B] 0.1 mm

C] <u>0.02 mm</u>

D] 0001 mm

187] Which laying out the vernier height gauge must be used on the
----

A] V block
B] Machine bed
C] Surface plate
D] Any flat surface

188] The part which is slides on the beam of a vernier height gauge is known as a ------

A] Base
B] Beam scale
C] Scriber
D] Vernier slide

189] The base of the vernier height gauge is generally made out of
----

A] Cast iron]
B] Steel
C] Aluminium alloy
D] Tungsten carbide

190] Which instrument iis used for marking layout?

A] Micrometer
B] Vernier
C] Depth gauge
D] Vernier height gauge

191] While marking with a Vernier height gauge, the work piece is generally ----------

A] Supported by an angle plate
B] Supported by another work piece
C] Held by one hand
D] Held without support

192] Which of the following is not the part of a combination set?

A] Stock
B] Square head
C] Protractor head
D] Centre head

Engineering Drawing in Petrochemical Engineering

18]The 'T' square is used for drawing lines ......

a] inclined
b] curved

c] vertical

d] <u>horizontal</u>

19] For drawing large size circle is drawn by.....

a] straight bar

b] <u>lengthening bar</u>

c] big bar

d] small bar

20] To draw or measure angle is used by.....

a]set square

b] <u>protractor</u>

c] 'T' square

d] none of these

21] The grade of pencil is used to sketching lettering ....

a] <u>conical point</u>

b] chisel point

c] soft

d] low

22] For drawing thin lines of uniform thickness the pencil should be sharpened in the form of ....

a] chisel edge

b]conical

c] <u>pointed</u>

d] none of these

23] What is used for drawing curves which can not drawn by compass

a] small compass

b] <u>French curve</u>

c] protractor

d] none of these

24]Unnecessary lines is removed by .....

a] Duster

b] sand paper block

c] <u>eraser</u>

d] none of these

25] Circle and arcs are drawn by means of .....l.

a] <u>compass</u>

b] divider

c] lengthening bar

d]none of these

26] Inking pen is used in drawing ......

a] horizontal line

b] non circular arcs

c] vertical lines

d] all of these

27] The card board scale are available in set of .....

a] 7

b] 8

c] 6

d] 9

28] The convenient length size of 30 -60°-90° set square for used in school and colleges are......

a] 250

b] 200

c] 300

d] none of these

29] Drawing board is shape of ....

a] square

b] rectangular

c] triangular

d] none of these

30] The 'T' square , set square ,scale protractor are complain use in.......

a] protractor

b] mini drafter

c] set square

d] none of these

31]Set square , T square edges are bevelled for the purpose of....

a] curve line

b] inking lines

b] taking measurements

d] none of these

32]Geometrical construction which are mostly based on plane geometry and which are very.......

a] Accuracy

b] Quality

c] Essential

d] Superior quality

33] How much method of drawing the regular polygons.......

a] Inscribe circle method and arc method
b] General method for drawing any polygon
c] Alternative method
d] All of these
34] The line AB can be divided into .... equal parts.
a] 7
b] 10
c] 15
d] All of them
35] Which method of constructing triangl in circle......
a] Inscribing
b] Describing
c] Both a and b
d] None of these
36] When two sides of the hexagon are required to be horizontal the starting point for stepping equal division should be on an end of the.....
a] Horizontal diameter
b] Vertical diameter
c] Inclined diameter
d] None of these
37] If two sides of hexagon are required to be vertical the starting point should be on an end of the....
a] Inclined diameter
b] Horizontal diameter
c] Vertical diameter
d] None of these
38] The section obtained by the inter section of the right circular cone by a plane in different position relative to the axis of the cone are called.......
a] Conics
b] Circles
c] Triangles
d] Half circle
39] When the section plane is inclined to the axis and cuts all the generators on one side on a apex the section is in......
a] Conic section
b] Ellipse
c] Parabola
d] Hyperbola

40] When the section plane is inclined to the axis and is parallel to one of the generators the section is a ....
a] Ellipse
b] <u>Parabola</u>
c] Hyperbola
d] Cycloid
41] Use of elliptical curve is........
a] Arches
b] Dams and monuments
c] Manholes, gland & stuffing boxes
d] <u>All of these</u>
42] Use of parabolic curve is.........
a] Bridges & arches
b] Sound reflectors
c] Light reflectors
d] <u>All of these</u>
43] Use of hyperbolical curve is......
a] <u>Cooling towers and water channel</u>
b] Dames
c] Bridges
d] All of these
44] When the point is within the circle, the curve is called an.......
a] Superior trochoid
b] <u>Interior trochoid</u>
c] Trochoid
d] Isotrochoid
45] When the point outside the circle then the curve is called as......
a] Interior trochoid
b] <u>Superior trochoid</u>
c] Trochoid
d] Insuperior trochoid
46] The curve general by a point on a circumference of a circle, which rolls without slipping along another circle it is called.......
a] <u>Epicycloids</u>
b] Hypocycloid
c] Involute
d] None of these
47] When the circle rolls inside another circle the curve is called.......

a] Hypocycloid
b] Epicycloids
c] Trochoid
d] <u>Hypotrochoid</u>
48] The use of archemedian spiral curve is made in........
a] Teeth profiles of helical gears
b] Profiles of cams
c] <u>Both a & b</u>
d] None of these
49] The cams are widely used in........
a] Automates
b] Printing machines
c] C engines
d] <u>All of these</u>
50] Spring index =
a] Diameter of coil / diameter of a wire
b] <u>Diameter of wire /diameter of coil</u>
c] Mean diameter of wire / diameter of coil
d] Mean diameter of a coil / diameter of wire
51] Eccentricity =
a] <u>Distance of a point from the focus / distance of the point from directrix</u>
b] Distance of focus from point / distance of point from
c] Distance of point from focus / distance of directrix of point
d] Distance of point from directrix / distance of point from focus
52] Mathematically an ellipse can be described by equation.....
a] $a^2 / X^2 + y^2 / b^2 = 1$
b] $x^2 / a^2 + y^2 / b^2$
c] $x^2 / a^2 + y^2 / b^2 = 0$
d] <u>$x^2 / a^2 + y^2 / b^2 = 1$</u>
53] Mathematically a parabola can be described by an equation......
a] $y^2 = 4ax$
b] $x^2 = 2ay$
c] $x^2 = 4ay$
d] <u>Both a & b</u>
54] Mathematically hyperbola can be described by an equation.......
a] <u>$x^2 /a^2 - y^2 /b^2 = 1$</u>
b] $x^2 /y^2 - y^2 /x^2 = 0$

c] Both a & b

d] None of these

55] Cycloid can be described by an equation......

a] y = a(1-cos Ø]

b] x = a(Ø -sin Ø]

c] Both a & b

d] None of these

56] The mathematically represented hypocycloid is.....

a] $Y = a \cos^3 Ø, X = a \sin^3 Ø$

b] $X = a \sin^3 Ø, Y = a \cos^3 Ø$

c] $X = a \cos^3 Ø, Y = a \sin^3 Ø$

d] None of these

57] Mathematically represented by involute is

a] $X = r \sin Ø - r Ø \cos Ø, Y = r \cos + r Ø \sin Ø$

b] $X = r \sin Ø + r \cos Ø, Y = r \cos Ø - r Ø \sin Ø$

c] $Y = r Ø \cos Ø - r \sin Ø, X = r \sin Ø - r Ø \cos Ø$

d] $X = r \cos Ø + r Ø \sin Ø, Y = r \sin Ø - r Ø \cos Ø$

58] The lines from the object to the plane are called.......

a] Projection

b] Projector

c] Reference plane

d] None of these

59] The orthographic projection an object is represented by View on the mutual perpendicular projection lines

a] Two or three

b] Three or two

c] Three or four

d] None of these

60] When the projectors are parallel to each other & also perpendicular to the plane, the projection is called......

a] Isometric projection

b] Oblique projection

c] Orthographic projection

d] Perspective projection

61] The two planes employed for the purpose of Orthographic projections are......

a] Auxillary plane

d] Horizontal plane

c] <u>Reference plane</u>
d] None of these

62] The line in which they intersect is termed the reference line & is denoted by the letters.......
a] AB
b] YZ
c] <u>XY</u>
d] None of these

63] The projection on the VP is called........
a] Side view
b] <u>Front view</u>
c] Top view
d] All of these

64] ....Method, when the views are drawn in their relative positions, the plane comes below the elevation. The view of the object as observed from the left-side the right of elevation.
a] Plane of projection
b] <u>First angle projection</u>
c] Third angle projection
d] None of these

65] Third angle projection method, the object is assumed to be situated in the........ quadrant.
a] First quadrant
b] Second quadrant
c] <u>Third quadrant</u>
d] Fourth quadrant

66] .... Method of projection is used in U.S.A .& also in other countries.
a] plane of projection
b] Orthographic projection
c] First-angle projection
d] <u>Third angle projection</u>

67] When an object is situated on the ground, in first angle projection method, the bottom of its ..... will co-inside with XY
a] Top view
b] <u>Front view</u>
c] side view
d] All of these

68] The important element of this projection system
a] An object
b] Plane of projection
c] An observer
d] All of these
69] When line AB is parallel to HP hence ....
a] It' front view to AB
b] It''s side view equal to AB
c] It's top view equal to AB
d] None of these
70] When a line is parallel to a plane; it's projection on plane is equal to it's ;
a] True length
b] True shape
c] True size
d] None of these
71] The point is parallel in which the line or line produced meet the point is plane is called it's ....
a] Line
b] ratio
c] Trace
d] none of these
72] .... is the shortest distance between two points.
a] a line
b] a point
c] a straight line
d] none of these
73] When the line intersect horizontal plane that's called.....
a] horizontal trace
b] vertical trace
c] trace of line
d] none of these
74]Planes may be divided into two main types ......
a] Perpendicular planes, auxillary planes
b] Perpendicular plane, oblique planes
c] Auxillary planes , perpendicular planes
d] none of these
75] Planes which are inclined to the reference plane are called......

a] Auxillary plane

b] <u>obliqeu plane</u>

c] Perpendicular planes

d] picture plane

76] When a plane is perpendicular to a reference plane it's projection on that plane is a...........

a] horizontal line

b] parallel line

c] <u>straight line</u>

d] none of these

77] When a plane is parallel to a reference plane , it's projection on that plane shows........

a] <u>It's true shape &size</u>

b] It's true length & size

c] It's true height & size

d] none of these

78] Plane perpendicular to VP & HP that plane is called as ....

a] Auxillary Plane

b] Oblique Plane

c] <u>Perpendicular Plane</u>

d] None of these

79] Perpendicular plane can be divides into the following types.........

a] Perpendicular to both the reference planes.

b] Perpendicular to one plane & parallel to other

c] Perpendicular to one plane & inclined to other

d] <u>All of these</u>

80] The planes have only two dimensions, viz........

a] <u>Length & breadth</u>

b] Length & height

c] Length & thickness

d] All of these

81] The imaginary line of prism joining the centrs of the bases called.........

a] Faces

b] <u>Axis</u>

c] Apex

d] Base

82] A right & regular prism has it's axis....... to the bases a] Parallel

b] <u>Perpendicular</u>

c] Inclined

d] None of these

83] When a pyramid or a cone is cut by a plane parallel to it's base thus removing the top portion, the remaining portion is called it's.........

a] Sphere

b] Cone

c] Cylinder

d] <u>Frustum</u>

84] Oblique cylinder & cones have their axes........ to their base

a] <u>Inclined</u>

b] Parallel

c] Perpendicular

d] All of these

85] Projection of two equal sphere s resting on the ground & in contact with each other, with the line joining there centre parallel to the..........

a] A VP

b] VP

c] <u>HP</u>

d] All of these

86] Projections of section on the other plane to which it is inclined is called.......

a] Section planes

b] <u>Apparent section</u>

c] True shape of sphere

d] None of these

87] When the section plane is parallel to the HP or the ground, the true shape of the section will be seen in.........

a] Front view

b] Side view

c] <u>Top view</u>

d] All of these

88] Surface of solid are laid out on a plane the figure obtained is called its........

a] Interpenetration

b] <u>Development</u>

c] Intersection

d] None of these

89] Development of surfaces is essential in.........

a] Foundry shop

b] <u>Sheet metal work</u>

c] Fitting shop

d] None of these

90] Which method of development used in transition pieces?

a] Parallel diameter

b] Radial line method

c] <u>Triangulation method</u>

d] Approximate method

91] Which method of development used in pyramids and cones.........

a] <u>Radial line method</u>

b] Parallel line method

c] Approximate method

d] Triangulation method

92] Parallel line method is used in..........

a] Prism

b] Cylinder

c] Cubes

d] <u>All of these</u>

93] Which method of development used in surface as sphere, paraboloid, ellipsoid, hyperboloid, and helicoids

a] Radial line method

b] Triangulation method

c] <u>Approximate method</u>

d] Parallel line method

94] Zone method and lune method is used in development of........

a] Prisms

b] Cones

c] <u>Sphere</u>

d] Pyramids

95] Calculation the subtended angle Θ by the formula $\Theta = 360^0 \times$ radius of the base circle

a] <u>Length of axis</u>

b] <u>Slant height</u>

c] Radius of axis

d] None of these

96] In engineering practice, objects constructed may have constituent part, the surfaces of which intersect one another in lines called........ of intersection.

a] <u>Lines</u>

b] Cones

c] Cylinder

d] Prisms

97] The line of interaction may be depending upon the nature of.......

a] <u>Intersection surface</u>

b] Intersecting solids

c] Intersection cones

d] None of these

98] The two plane surface intersect in a........ line

a] Curve

b] <u>Straight</u>

c] Plane

d] All of these

99] The line of intersection between two curved surface or between......... Surface and a curved surface is a curve.

a] A curved

b] <u>A plane</u>

c] A solids

d] None of these

100] When a solids completely penetration another solids there will be two lines of intersection. These lines are sometimes called the line or........

a] Line of interpenetration

b] <u>Curve of interpenetration</u>

c] Solids of interpenetration

d] All of these

101] Use of penetration curve is.......

a] Sheet metal work

b] Fitting shop

c] <u>Fabricating work</u>

d] Foundry shop

102] Methods of determining the line of intersection between surface of two interpenetration.........

a] Approximate method & radial line method

b] <u>Line method and cutting plane method</u>

c] Triangulation method and parallel line method

d] None of these

103] Example of interpenetration is..........

a] Two prism intersection

b] Cylinder and prism intersection

c] Cone and cylinders intersection

d] All of these

104] Two cylinder intersection is example of.........

a] Intersection

b] Interpenetration

c] Cone intersection

d] None of these

105] .... Method is explained in detail while solving illustrative problems

a] Line method

b] Radial line method

c] Cutting plane method

d] Parallel line method

106] What is a type of isometric projection?

a] Pictorial projection

b] Orthographic projection

c] Perspective projection

d] Oblique Projection

107] Isometric views have been drawn........

a] Full scale

b] Half scale

c] True length

d] True scale

108] The line parallel to isometric axis are called........

a] Isometric axis

b] Isometric line

c] Isometric planes

d] Isometric views

109] The isometric projection is reduce in the ratio.........

a] 3 :

b] 1 : 2

c] 2 : 2

d] 2 : 3

110] The isometric projection of circle drawn with........
a] Isometric Plane
b] Isometric graph
c] Isometric Drawing
d] <u>Isometric Scale</u>
111] The major axis of the ellipse is long than...............
a] Radius of the circle
b] True diameter
c] <u>Diameter of the circle</u>
d] None of these
112] Makes practice for drawing of isometric view using........
a] Isometric planes
b] Isometric lines
c] <u>Isometric graph</u>
d] Isometric view
113] Use of parabolic curve is
a] <u>Sound reflectors</u>
b] Dams
c] Man hole of boiler
d] Gland & stuffing box
114] When the section plane is inclined the true shape of section on
a] AVP
b] VP
c] HP
d] <u>A/P</u>
115] When section plane is perpendicular to both the HP & VP the true shape of section on
a]Top view
b] <u>Side view</u>
c] Front view
d]None of this
116] When view projected on auxiliary planes are called
a] <u>Auxiliary view</u>
b Sectional view
c] Front view
d] None of these
117] Invisible features of an object are shown by means of
a] Outline

b] Chain lines

c] <u>Hidden lines</u>

d] None of these

118] Importance of sectional view on drawing for

a] <u>Internal details</u>

b] Outer details

c] Hatching

d] None of these

119] The component is cut by a straight cutting plane is divided in to two parts

a] Half section

b] <u>Full section</u>

c] Offset section

d] Removed section

120] section line is two different parts (pieces] in contact should be drown in...

a] Same direction

b] <u>Opposite direction</u>

c]parallel direction

d] None of these

121] When area to be sectioned in very small as for this plate and structural members blacked in section may be used. A space of not less than

a] 0.07mm

b] <u>0.7mm</u>

c] 0.05mm

d] 0.5mm

122] The sum of interior angles of polygon is equal

a] <u>(2*n-4]*Right angle</u>

b] (2*n]*Right angle-4

c] (2*4-n]*Right angle

d] (2-4*n]*Right angle

123] One micron is equal to ....mm

a] <u>0.001</u>

b] 1000

c] 0.01

d] 0.1

124] Development of surface is essential in.....

a] foundry shop

b] <u>sheet metal work</u>
c] fitting shop
d] none of these
125] Which method of development used in transition piece?
a] parallel line method
b] radial line method
c] <u>triangulation method</u>
d] none of these
126] The isometric projection is reduced in the ratio of
a] $\sqrt{2}:\sqrt{3}$
b] $\sqrt{3}:\sqrt{2}$
c] $1:\sqrt{2}$
d] <u>none of these</u>
127] When measurements are required in three units the scale is used....
a] full scale
b] plain scale
c] half scale
d] <u>none of these</u>
128]Isometric drawing is larger in production about isometric projection is....
a] <u>22.5%</u>
b] <u>0.815</u>
c] 9/11
d] none of these
129] While isometric of sphere of spherical parts.......is must be used.
a] full scale
b] <u>isometric length</u>
c] true length
d] half scale
130] When circle draw with isometric scale the length of major axis of the ellipse to the ....
a] <u>true diameter</u>
b] isometric diameter
c] isometric diameter
d] none of these
131] In isometric view which contain a large number of non –isometric lines which method is used
a] box method

b] off-set method

c] <u>co-ordinate method</u>

d] centre lay out method

132] When drawing is drawn smaller than actual size of object .....

a] full scale

b] enlarging scale

c] <u>reducing scale</u>

d] none of these

133] When e=1 curve is called.....

a] <u>parabola</u>

b] hyperbola

c] ellipse

d] none of these

134]Compare with isometric drawing the advantage of oblique projection is....

a] <u>front face is in true shape</u>

b] two axis are always perpendicular to each othe

c] receding axis is taken at some convenient angles

d] none of these

135]If all the receding edges are drawn true length the oblique projection is called...

a] <u>cavilier projection</u>

b] cabinet projection

c] general projection

d] none of these

136] The large object such as building the point is usually taken height of .....

a] 0.8mm

b] 1.2mm

c] <u>1.8mm</u>

d] 1.5mm

137] Central plane is the imaginary vertical plane which passes through....

a] <u>P. P</u>

b] H.L

c] G.P

d] C.P

138] When object is parallel to P.P the perspective is called......

a] <u>one point</u>
b] two point
c] three point
d] none of these
139] The line drawn through the station point from the picture plane shall be ....
a] <u>P.A</u>
b] H.L
c] G.L
d] C
140] The distance of the station point from the picture plane shall be .....
a] Max. Diameter of the object
b] <u>Twice the max. Diameter of the object</u>
c] Half the max. Diameter of the object
d] none of these
141] In isometric view of hexagonal plane all the sides of hexagon is .....
a] equal length
b] <u>unequal length</u>
c] none of these
142] When all the faces are equal & regular the polyhedron is said....
a] <u>regular</u>
b] prisms
c] irregular
d] pyramid
143] Oblique prisms &pyramid have ......
a] axis perpendicular to the base
b] <u>axis inclined to the base</u>
c] faces inclined to the H.P
d] none of these
144] Icosahedrons has equal equilateral triangular faces
a] 12
b] 8
c] <u>20</u>
d] 6
145] When a pyramid or cone is cut by a plane parallel to its base is called.....
a] pyramid
b] turned carted

c] frustum

d] none of these

146] Plane which are inclined to both the reference plane is called ......

a] oblique plane

b] perpendicular plane

c] inclined plane

d] none of these

147] When a line parallel to H.P & perpendicular to V.P the trace line is.....

a] V.T

b] H.T

c] no trace

d] V.T& H.T

148] When a line parallel to the V.P and inclined to H.P the true length of line in.....

a] front view

b] top view

c] side view

d] none of these

149] When point situated in front quadrant

a] above the H.P & in front of V.P

b] below the H.P & in front of V.P

c] behind the V.P & above H.P

d] below the H.P & behind the V.P

150] Find the quadrant of point "b" is 15 mm above H.P and 25mm behind the V.P

a] I st

b] III rd

c] IIII th

d] II nd

151] In first angle projection front view is ......

a] above the top view

b] below the top view

c] above the side view

d] below the side view

152] In orthographic projection the projectors are ....

a] parallel to plane

b] perpendicular to plane

c] inclined to plane

d] none of these

153] L.H.S.V means.........

a] length of side view

b] left hand view

c] right hand view

d] <u>left hand side view</u>

154] The object lines between the observer and the plane of projection is ....

a] 3rd angle

b] <u>1st angle</u>

c] 4th angle

d] 2nd angle

155] In third angle projection plane of projection is assumed to be ......

a] non transparent

b] quadrant

c] <u>transparent</u>

d] dihedral angle

156] In third angle projection top view is always on......

a] <u>above front view</u>

b] above top view

c] below the front view

d] below the side view

157] Four quadrants which may be called as......

a] anticlockwise

b] first and third angle

c] <u>dihedral angles</u>

d] none of these

158] In first angle projection method the view see from the left is placed on .....

a] left of the front view

b] <u>right of front view</u>

c] above the top view

d] below the front view

159] The size of A2 paper is .....

a] 297*420

b] 594*841

c] <u>420*594</u>

d] 210*297

160] The edge of board on which 'T' square is sli9ding is called ......

a] straight edge

b] <u>working edge</u>

c] chisel edge

d] none of these

161] The size of title block as recommended by B.I.S . is .....

a] <u>185*65</u>

b] 150*50

c] 170*65

d] none of these

162] For A2 size sheet the number of zones suggested by B.I.S. along the length & width.......

a] 12,8

b] 16,12

c] 8,6

d] none of these

163] The drawing sheet is so folded that...... is always on the top.

a] drawing

b] lettering

c] title block

d] none of these

164] In free hand sketching horizontal lines are sketched from.......

a] right to left

b] up to down

c] left to right

d] none of these

165] When drawing is down smaller than actual size of object

a] enlarging scale

b] reducing scale

c] full scale

d] none of these

166] The ratio of the length of the object represented on drawing to the actual length of object is called.......

a] full scale

b] R.F.

c] half scale

d] plain scale

167] When measurements are required in three unit the scale is used.....

a] full scale

b] half scale

c] plain scale

d] none of these

168] When protractor is not available the scale of chord is used ......

a] measure length

b] measure angle

c] measure scale

d] none of these

169] The least count of a vernier calliper is ....

a] 0.001

b] <u>0.02</u>

c] 0.001

d] 0.0002

170] Which scale is used to read a very small unit with great accuracy?

a] plain scale

b] <u>diagonal scale</u>

c] scale of chord

d] vernier scale

171] The R.F. is greater than one (1] the scale is ....

a] plain scale

b] diagonal scale

c] <u>enlarging scale</u>

d] reducing scale

Electrical MCQ for Petrochemical Engineering

85] A heater draws a current of 8A when connected to a 240V source] What is the resistance value of the heater element in ohms?

A] 40

B] 20

C] <u>30</u>

D] 60

86] An electric soldering iron with an 80 ohms heating element is plugged into a 240V outlet] How much current will be drawn by the iron?

A] 2A

B] <u>3A</u>

C] 4A

D] 5A

87] The alternator in a car delivers 4A and has a load of 3 ohms connected across its terminals] Find the voltage of the circuit

A] 18V

B] 24V

C] <u>12V</u>

D] 16V

88] Three resistors of 1K ohms, 2K ohms and 7K ohms are connected in series with a 30 V supply] If 2 K ohms and 7 K ohms resistors are open circuited, a voltmeter connected across the 7K ohms resistor will indicate...

A] 10 k ohms, 3A

B] 10 k ohms, 300mA

C] <u>10 k ohms, 3 mA</u>

D] 5 k ohms, 6 mA

89] A voltage source produces an IR drop of 40V across a 20 ohms resistance, 60V across a 30 ohms resistance and 180V across a 90 ohms resistance all in series] How much is the applied voltage?

A] 180 V

B] 240 V

C] 100 V

D] <u>280 V</u>

90] Three resistors 27 ohms, 47 ohms and 68 ohms are connected in parallel] What is the otal resistance?

A] <u>less than 27 ohms</u>

B] greater than 68 ohms

C] between 27 and 47 ohms

D] sum of all the three resistances

91] One million and one mege ohms resistors are there if connected both in parallel, what would be the combined resistance value?

A] <u>0.5 mega ohm</u>

B] 0.5 milli ohm

C] 0.5 kilo ohm

D] 0.5 ohm

92] A 24 ohms and a 8 ohms resistors in parallel gets a combined resistance of...

A] <u>6 ohms</u>

B] 12 ohms

C] 3 ohms

D] 32 ohms

93] Resistors of the following values are connected in parallel, 5 ohms, 5 kilo-ohms, 50 kilo-ohms, 5 mega ohms] Their equivalent resistance will be very near to...

A] 4.5 ohms
B] 4500 ohms
C] 45000 ohms
D] 4,500,000 ohms

94] The resistance of given wire is 2 ohms] The resistance of the other wire made of the same material having twice the length and twice the cross sectional area is...

A] 5 ohms
B] 6 ohms
C] 2 ohms
D] 8 ohms

95] If the area of a metal wire of a given length is doubles, its resistance will...

A] be doubled
B] be halved
C] remain the same
D] be four times more

96].Among the following only one is regarded as resistance wire

A] gold
B] silver
C] nichrome
D] copper

97] Arc heating occurs when the air between electrodes of opposite polarity becomes..

A] moistened
B] dry
C] ionized
D] none of the above

98] The meter used to measure the temperature of furnace is...

A] hydrometer
B] pyrometer
C] hygrometer
D] tachometer

99] in the case of electrolyte a rise in temperature causes...

A] decrease in resistance

B] increase in resistance

C] no change in resistance

D] none of the above

100] Heat developed in a conductor is proportional to the...

A] square of the power

B] square of the resistance

C] square of the current

D] square of the time

101] Out of the four metal/alloys given below, one has almost no change in resistance for temperature change...

A] nickel

B] nichrome

C] platinum

D] manganin

102] A material that is slightly repelled by a magnet is called ...

A] magnetic

B] paramagnetic

C] diamagnetic

D] ferromagnetic

103] A material that can be magnetized only very slightly is called...

A] magnetic

B] paramagnetic

C] diamagnetic

D] ferromagnetic

104] Substances that can be magnetized easily and make very strong magnets are called...

A] ferromagnetic

B] diamagnetic

C] paramagnetic

D] permanent magnetic

105] A substance that has a high retentivity can be used for the manufacture of...

A] electromagnets

B] permanent magnets

C] temporary magnets

D] paramagnets

106] A substance that has low retentivity can be used for the manufacture of...

A] <u>electromagnets</u>

B] permanent magnets

C] bar magnets

D] paramagnets

107] The symbol for inductance is...

A] H

B] I

C] <u>L</u>

D] X

108] Tube lamp choke is the best example of...

A] open circuited

B] <u>short circuited</u>

C] grounded

D] connected to the neutral line

109] The initial function of a choke in a tube light circuit is to...

A] limit the starting current

B] <u>induce high voltage</u>

C] heat up the filament

D] limit the current after starting

110] The second function of a choke in a tube light circuit is to...

A] limit the starting current

B] induce high voltage

C] heat up the filament

D] <u>limit the current after starting</u>

111] The periodic time of a wave from is 2ms] Calculate the frequency

A] 50 HZ

B] 5 HZ

C] <u>500HZ</u>

D] 5 KHZ

112] How big is the peak amplitude of a sine-wave with an effective value of 220 volts?

A] <u>311 V</u>

B] 380 V

C] 400 V

D] 440 V

113] The peak-to-peak voltage is 99V] how big is the effective value of the sine wave?

A] 70 V

B] 44.5V

C] 49.5 V

D] <u>35 V</u>

114] A moving coil voltmeter reads 10 V AC] How big is the effective voltage?

A] higher

B] lower

C] <u>the same</u>

D] 10% higher

115] A moving iron ammeter reads 10 A] how big is the peak current of the oscillation?

A] 7.07 A

B] 1.1414A

C] 70.7 A

D] <u>14.1 A</u>

116] A current of 2 amps flows through a resistance of 10 ohms] The power dissipated in the resistance is equal to...

A] 20 watts

B] 200 watts

C] <u>40 watts</u>

D] 5 watts

117] If the frequency changes from 50 HZ to 100 HZ keeping voltage constant, the inductive reactance of coil connected to supply...

A] remains same

B] become half

C] <u>become doubled</u>

D] become 4 times

118] Capacitance is not affected by...

A] plate area

B] distance between plates

C] dialectic material

D] <u>frequency</u>

119] The capacitive reactance of a capacitor varies...

A] directly with frequency

B] <u>inversely with frequency</u>

C] directly with applied voltage

D] inversely with applied voltage

120] A capacitor acquired 3 coulombs of charge when 6 volts are applied across it] It has a capacitance of ...

A] 0.5 farad

B] 3 farads

C] 3 farads

D] 18 farads

121] A capacitor is connected across a 200 volt AC line, its minimum voltage rating should be...

A] 100 volts

B] 200 Volts

C] 300 volts

D] 400 volts

122] when testing a capacitor with an ohmmeter, the meter indicates some resistance] The capacitor under test is...

A] leaky

B] open

C] good

D] short

123] The total capacitance of a 40 micro farad capacitor connected in series with an 80 micro farad capacitor is...

A] 26.7 micro farad

B] 40 micro farad

C] 60.6 micro farad

D] 120 micro farad

124] For obtaining 1 micro farad capacitor from 3 nos] of 3 micro farad capacitors we have to connect...

A] all in parallel

B] all in series

C] 2 series and one in parallel

D] none of the above

125] In an AC series circuit having R and C the current flowing through the capacitor will be...

A] lagging the voltage

B] leading the voltage

C] in phase with the voltage

D] none of the above

126] If the frequency of the supply is increased in the R-C series circuit the capacitive reactance will be

A] <u>reduced</u>

B] increased

C] having no effect

D] none of the above

127] Power companies are interested in improving the power factor to

A] <u>reduce line current</u>

B] increase motor efficiency

C] increase volt-amperes

D] decrease power

128] A capacitor increases the power factor value of an AC motor load when it is connected...

A] in series with the motor

B] in series with the starter

C] <u>in parallel with the motor</u>

D] in series with the main winding

129] Normally, the power factor of an incandescent lighting circuit is..

A] 0

B] 0.5

C] 0.707

D] <u>1.0</u>

130] When resistance alone is used to determine current in an RLC series circuit, the circuit is...

A] an inductive circuit

B] a capacitive circuit

C] a combination circuit

D] <u>a resonant circuit</u>

131] Inductive reactance is directly related to..

A] resistance

B] <u>frequency</u>

C] capacitance

D] power

132] Synchronous motor when used for power factor improvement should be...

A] under excited

B] <u>over excited</u>

C] loaded

D] running at no load

133] In a RL parallel circuit, the opposition to total current is called...

A] reactance

B] resistance

C] a vector sum

D] <u>impedance</u>

134] In a AC parallel RL circuit, the power dissipated at the

A] impedance

B] <u>resistance</u>

C] inductance

D] capacitance

135] How much is the nominal output voltage of a carbon zinc cell?

A] 12V

B] <u>1.5V</u>

C] 2.0V

D] 2.2V

136] Cells are connected in series to..

A] <u>increase the output voltage</u>

B] decreases the output voltage

C] decrease the internal resistance

D] increase the current capacity

54137connected in

A] series

B] <u>parallel</u>

C] series-parallel

D] parallel-series

138] The capacity of a cell is measured in

A] watt-hour

B] watts

C] amperes

D] <u>ampere-hour</u>

139] The primary cell which has the shortest shelf life is

A] <u>carbon – zinc</u>

B] alkaline

C] mercury

D] lithium

140] The cell which has very high energy density for given weight or volume to

A] carbon-zinc

B] alkaline

C] mercury

D] lithium

141] A 100-Ah capacity battery should deliver a current of 8A for approximately...

A] 12 h

B] 8 h

C] 20 h

D] 100 h

142] When the battery is needed to be kept idle for a long time...

A] overcharge the battery

B] remove electrolyte

C] clean the plates with distilled water

D] dry them and store the battery in cool dry clean place

143] The active materials of the nickel iron cell are...

A] nickel hydroxide

B] powdered iron and its oxide

C] 21% solution of caustic potash

D] all the above materials

144] The capacity of a cell is measured in

A] watt hour

B] watts

C] amperes

D] ampere-hour

145] To charge a secondary cell, the system used is

A] low voltage AC

B] high voltage AC

C] AC

D] DC

146] What is the number of phases in a normal industrial supply system?

A] one

B] three

C] four

D] two

147] In a 3 phase star connected alternator, the coils have a phase difference of...

A] 120°

B] 240°

C] 60°

D] 360∘

148] Delta connection is used no one of the following

A] primary of the transmission line transformer

B] alternator winding

C] secondary of the distribution transformer

D] <u>primary of the distribution transformer</u>

149] Which method can be used to measure the power in a 3-phase unbalanced load system?

A] one wattmeter method

B] <u>tow wattmeter method</u>

C] three wattmeter method

D] three ammeter method

150] Two wattmeters can be used to measure 3-hase power in a 3-phase, 3 wire system with...

A] balanced load

B] unbalanced load

C] <u>balanced as well as unbalanced load</u>

D] out of balanced load

151] A single wattmeter can be used to measure power in a 3-phase system only when the load is..

A] <u>balanaced</u>

B] unbalanced

C] balanced as well as unbalanced load

D] constant

152] The force producing movement of the pointer in an indicating instrument is called as...

A] <u>deflecting force</u>

B] controlling force

C] damping force

D] distracting force

153] A permanent magnet moving coil instrument will read...

A] only AC quantities

B] <u>only DC quantities</u>

C] both AC and DC quantities

D] pulsating quantities

154] An instrument using gravity control will read correctly if used in..

A] <u>vertical position only</u>

B] horizontal position only

C] inclined position only

D] any position

155] Which one of the following damping methods is used in permanent magnet moving coil instrument?

A] air damping

B] fluid damping

C] spring damping

D] eddy current damping

156] Moving coil instrument works on the effect of...

A] chemical effect

B] heating effect

C] electrostatic effect

D] electromagnetic effect

157] The meter installed at your house to measure electrical energy is an example of...

A] indication type instrument

B] recording type instrument

C] indicating as well as recording type instrument

D] integrating type instrument

158].Which of the following material is preferred for permanent magnet?

A] alnico

B] y-alloy

C] silicon steel

D] wrought iron

159] The instrument which could be classified as absolute instrument is...

A] milli ammeter

B] micro ammeter

C] galvanometer

D] tangent galvanomer

160] Which of the following methods of damping is commonly used in moving iron instrument?

A] Air damping

B] fluid damping

C] eddy current damping

D] viscosity damping

161] The deflecting torque of a moving iron instrument is directly proportional to the..

A] current

B] <u>square of the current</u>

C] square root of the current

D] voltage

162]Which of the following is used for measuring the medium resistance directly?

A] ammeter

B] <u>megger</u>

C] ohmmeter

D] voltmeter

163] An ohmmeter is used for measuring the...

A] insulation resistance

B] <u>resistance</u>

C] current

D] potential difference

164] Which of the following components is not a part of an ohmmeter?

A] fixed resistor

B] variable resistor

C] <u>capacitor</u>

D] battery

165] In shunt ohmmeter, maximum deflection signifies ..

A] <u>maximum resistance</u>

B] minimum resistance

C] a fault in the megger

D] none of these

166].An unknown DC voltage is to be measured, which measuring range will you select first?

A] <u>500V</u>

B] 50V

C] 1.5 V

D] 0.5V

167].An unknown direct current of micro ampere rating is to be measured, which measuring range will you select first?

A] 20 micro amp

B] 15 micro amp

C] 150 micro amp

D] <u>500 micro amp</u>

168] A multimeter cannot measure...

A] current

B] potential difference

C] <u>capacitance</u>

D] resistance

169] Dynamometer type meters are used to measure...

A] only AC quantities

B] <u>only DC quantities</u>

C] both AC and DC

D] pulsating AC only

170] Which effect is used in wattmeter?

A] <u>electrodynamic effect</u>

B] thermal effect

C] chemical effect

D] electrostatic effect

171] Which of the instrument listed below operates efficiently as wattmeter in both AC and DC?

A] PMMC instrument

B] <u>dynamometer instrument</u>

C] hot wire instrument

D] MI instrument

172] Electrodynamic type of instrument are used commonly for the measurement of...

A] voltage

B] current

C] resistance D]

173] When the phase and neutral of the energy meter are interchanged, its disc...

A] <u>rotates in reverse direction</u>

B] rotates in correct direction

C] will stop

D] rotates slowly

E] rotates at high speed

174] When the disc of energy meter is rotating even without connecting any load, the error is called

A] <u>creeping error</u>

B] phase error

C] friction error

D] temperature error

175] AC single phase energy meters record the energy in the unit of...

A] kilowatt hours

B] number of thousands of disc rotation

C] volt amperes

D] kilo volt ampere

176] A megger measures resistance in...

A] ohms

B] hundreds of ohms

C] thousands of ohms

D] millions of ohms

177] A megger is exclusively designed for measuring..

A] very high resistance

B] very low resistance

C] ground faults in power lines

D] over loads on DC motors

178] For pipe earthing the minimum internal diameter of galvanized iron of steel pipe required is...

A] 12.5 mm

B] 16mm

C] 3.5 mm

D] 4 m

179] The earth conductor provides a path to ground for..

A] leakage current

B] over current

C] high voltage

D] circuit current

180] if the size of the circuit copper conductor is 10 sq-mm then the size of earth conductor in G.I] wire should be...

A] 1.5 sq.mm

B] 2.5 sq.mm

C] 5 sq.mm

D] 10 sq.mm

181] One calory is equal to,,,

A] 4187 joules

B] 418.7 joules

C] 41.87 joules

D] <u>4.187 joules</u>

182] The operating temperature range of electrical stove with bare heating element is...

A] 300° to 400°C

B] 500° to 600°C

C] <u>550° to 900°C</u>

D] 1100° to 1300°C

183] Which appliance works on heating effect of electric current?

A] incandescent lamp

B] bimetallic thermostat

C] H R C fuse

D] <u>toaster</u>

184] What is the size of nichrome wire for heating element of 1000 watts, 230V heater at 500°C?

A] 18 SWG

B] 20SWG

C] <u>24 SWG</u>

D] 25 SWG

185] The heat proof insulating material used for heater base is...

A] mica

B] <u>porcelain</u>

C] asbestos

D] glass wool

186].The temperature regulating component of an automatic electric iron is...

A] heating element

B] <u>thermostat</u>

C] sole plate

D] pressure plate

187].The bread toasting zone temperature is about...

A] 400°C

B] 800°C

C] <u>260°C</u>

D] 975°C

188] If a winding makes electrical contact with the metal case of the mixer motor the winding is...

A] <u>grounded</u>

B] open circuited

C] short circuited

D] loose connected

189] If the end shafts of a rotor turns blue it is an indication of...

A] scoring

B] <u>overheating</u>

C] freezing

D] burring

190] What type of motor is used in a food mixer?

A] DC shunt motor

B] <u>universal motor</u>

C] capacitor start motor

D] capacitor start and run motor

191] In what position is the motor mounted in most of the mixers?

A] <u>vertical</u>

B] horizontal

C] inclined

D] parallel

Petroleum Engineering MCQ for Petrochemical Engineering

1. With increase in the number of carbon and hydrogen atoms in hydrocarbon molecules, the density of petroleum products

(A) Decreases

(B) <u>Increases</u>

(C) Remain same

(D) Unpredictable from the data

2. Which is the most ideal feed stock for 'coking' process used for the manufacture of petroleum coke?

(A) Naphtha

(B) <u>Vacuum residue</u>

(C) Light gas oil

(D) Diesel

3. Feedstock for the production of biodiesel is

(A) Herbal plants

(B) <u>Used vegetable oils</u>

(C) LSHS

(D) Bagasse

4. Which of the following has maximum hydrogen/carbon ratio (by weight)?

(A) Naphtha
(B) <u>Gasoline</u>
(C) Diesel
(D) Fuel oil

5. Methyl tertiary butyl ether (MTBE), a high octane (octane no. = 115) gasoline blending component is produced by the simple additive reaction of isobutylene with
(A) <u>Methyl alcohol</u>
(B) Ethyl alcohol
(C) Methane
(D) Ethane

6. The first crude oil refinery of India is located at
(A) Naharkatiya
(B) <u>Digboi</u>
(C) Kochi
(D) Madras

7. CnH2n is the general formula for
(A) Olefins
(B) Naphthenes
(C) <u>Both (a) and (b)</u>
(D) Neither (a) nor (b)

8. The general formula of naphthenes is
(A) CnH2n + 2
(B) <u>CnH2n-6 (where, n ≥ 6)</u>
(C) CnHn-4
(D) Same as that for olefins i.e. CnH2n

9. Carbon percentage (by weight) in crude petroleum may be about
(A) 65
(B) 75
(C) <u>85</u>
(D) 95

10. Solvent used for dewaxing of petroleum products are
(A) Furfural
(B) Methyl ethyl ketone (MEK)
(C) <u>Propane</u>
(D) Both (b) & (c)

11. In catalytic cracking, the
(A) Gasoline obtained has a very low octane number

(B) Pressure & temperature is very high

(C) <u>Gasoline obtained has very high aromatic content</u>

(D) Gasoline obtained has very high amount of gum forming compounds

12. Petroleum liquid fuels having flash point greater than 66°C is considered as safe during storage and handling. Which of the following has flash point > 66°C?

(A) Naphtha

(B) Petrol

(C) Kerosene

(D) <u>Heavy fuel oil</u>

13. Pressure & temperature maintained in catalytic cracking is about

(A) <u>2 atm & 500°C</u>

(B) 10 atm & 500°C

(C) 30 atm & 200°C

(D) 50 atm & 750°C

14. An upper limit of oil content is limited to about ___________ percent for achieving efficient and satisfactory level of wax sweating.

(A) 5

(B) 15

(C) <u>40</u>

(D) 60